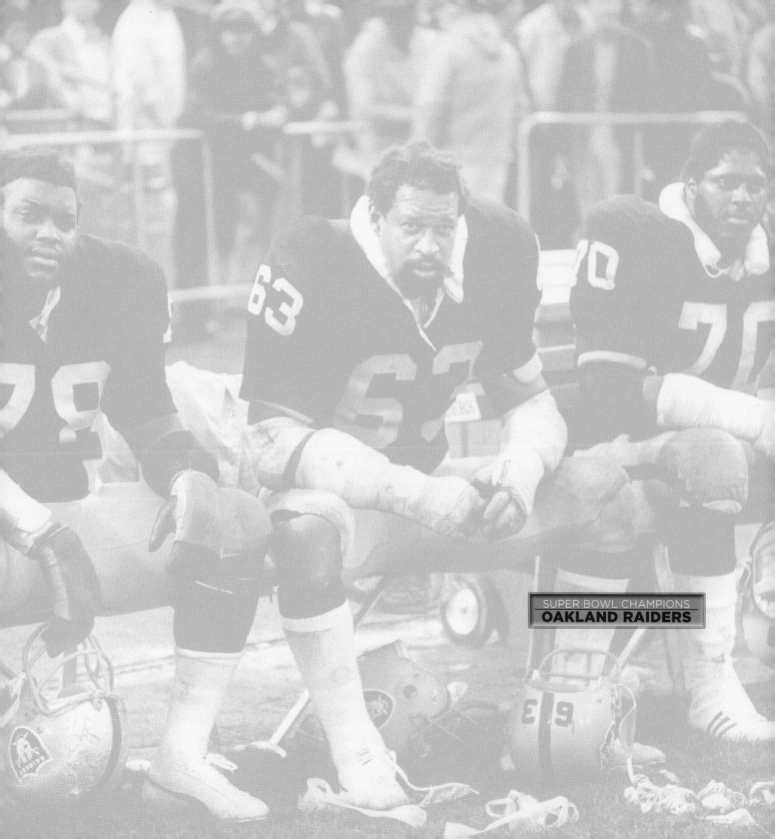

DEFENSIVE BACK
TYVON BRANCH

SUPER BOWL CHAMPIONS

OAKLAND RAIDERS

AARON FRISCH

CREATIVE EDUCATION

Published by Creative Education
P.O. Box 227, Mankato, Minnesota 56002
Creative Education is an imprint of The Creative Company
www.thecreativecompany.us

Design and production by Blue Design
Art direction by Rita Marshall
Printed in the United States of America

Photographs by Corbis (Bettmann), Getty Images (B. Bennett, Bernstein Associates, Kevin C. Cox, John Elk III, James Flores/NFL Photos, Focus on Sport, Otto Greule Jr., Jed Jacobsohn, John G. Mabanglo/AFP, Ronald C. Modra/Sports Imagery, NFL, Mike Powell, Thomas B. Shea, Greg Trott, Michael Zagaris)

Library of Congress Cataloging-in-Publication Data
Frisch, Aaron.
Oakland Raiders / Aaron Frisch.
p. cm. — (Super bowl champions)
Includes index.
Summary: An elementary look at the Oakland Raiders professional football team, including its formation in 1960, most memorable players, Super Bowl championships, and stars of today.
ISBN 978-1-60818-384-5
1. Oakland Raiders (Football team)—History—Juvenile literature. I. Title.

GV956.O24F75 2014
796.332'640979466—dc23   2013014833

First Edition
9 8 7 6 5 4 3 2 1

OFFENSIVE LINEMAN
ROBERT GALLERY

HOWIE LONG / 1981–93

Howie was a big defensive end who was hard to block. He led the Raiders' defense for 13 seasons.

TABLE OF CONTENTS

JOHN MADDEN / 1969–78

John was a coach who led the Raiders to their first championship. Later, he worked on TV.

THE ROWDY RAIDERS

When Oakland, California, got a football team, its owners wanted a name that sounded tough. "Raiders" is another name for pirates. The Oakland Raiders set sail!

WILLIE BROWN / 1967-78

Willie was a fast cornerback who made 39 **interceptions** for Oakland. That is a team **record**.

PARC OAKLA

JL
inn

SCOTT'S
SEAFOOD

Cafe

SCOTT'S SEAFOOD

WELCOME TO OAKLAND

Oakland is a **port** city by the Pacific Ocean. It is close to a bigger city called San Francisco. Besides the Raiders, Oakland has a baseball team called the Athletics.

JIM OTTO / 1960-74

Jim was one of the first Raiders stars. He was a tough center who wore number 00 on his jersey.

SILVER AND BLACK

The Raiders are the only National Football League (NFL) team whose main color is black. Many Raiders fans wear black and silver clothing.

DEFENSIVE END
BEN DAVIDSON

15

FRED BILETNIKOFF

THE RAIDERS' STORY

The Raiders started playing in 1960. They were part of the American Football League (AFL) then. The Raiders soon hired a smart coach named Al Davis. Wide receiver Fred Biletnikoff helped the Raiders get better. Fred hardly ever dropped passes. After the 1976 season, the Raiders won their first Super Bowl!

AL DAVIS

MARCUS ALLEN / 1982–92

Marcus was one of the greatest Raiders running backs. He used slick moves to get away from tacklers.

After the 1980 season, quarterback Jim Plunkett helped Oakland beat the Philadelphia Eagles to win the Super Bowl again. It was a big **upset**!

"I really thought I was going to be the savior, but all I did was put more pressure on myself."
— JIM PLUNKETT

TIM BROWN

**DEFENSIVE END
LYLE ALZADO**

The Raiders moved to the city of Los Angeles in 1982. They won Super Bowl XVIII (18) the next year. In 1995, the Raiders moved back to Oakland.

The Raiders had some good seasons in the 1990s. Wide receiver Tim Brown helped Oakland get to the Super Bowl after the 2002 season. But the Raiders lost.

SEBASTIAN JANIKOWSKI / 2000–present

Sebastian was a kicker with a powerful left leg. He made many long field goals for the Raiders.

JANIKOWSKI: *jan-ih-KOW-skee*

In 2013, Oakland fans cheered for players like Darren McFadden. Darren was one of the NFL's fastest running backs. The Raiders hoped to soon fight their way to another Super Bowl!

DARREN McFADDEN

21

FACTS FILE

CONFERENCE/DIVISION:
American Football
Conference, West Division

TEAM COLORS:
Black and silver

HOME STADIUM:
Oakland-Alameda County
Coliseum

SUPER BOWL VICTORIES:
XI, January 9, 1977
  32–14 over Minnesota
  Vikings
XV, January 25, 1981
  27–10 over Philadelphia
  Eagles
XVIII, January 22, 1984
  38–9 over Washington
  Redskins

NFL WEBSITE FOR KIDS:
http://nflrush.com

LINEBACKER ROLANDO McCLAIN

23

GLOSSARY

interceptions — plays in which a defensive player catches a pass thrown by the other team

port — a city by an ocean or big lake where ships pick up and drop off things

record — something that is the most or best ever

upset — a game in which the team that most people think will win ends up losing

INDEX